## *POETIC PLAGUE*

*Author: P.S. Harrison*

*Dear reader,*

*Life is poetry, and within poetry there is life. This book is a representation of life itself; many may ask why not a novel? Poetry for me is a novel itself telling the unsaid and the said, one should read between the lines and unlock their third eye with true intentions to grasp the memories of life and beyond. Breath has given me the inspiration to write this book as the aura of others gave me the emotional intelligence to paint a vivid image of the emotions many can't describe. Death, nature, love, hate, deceit and regret are things we all face during this journey on a road we call life. The roads will be rough, smooth, dark or ignited, it is up to you how well you want to walk the roads of life and what memory or impact one will possibly leave. To you my dearest reader never be afraid to live the life you deserve, journey on to the roads of life; knowledge and wisdom is strength. Be the best you— even when persons see the worst. Do enjoy my emotional journey.*

*P.S Harrison*

## Table of Contents

| | |
|---|---:|
| Alpha bet | 1 |
| Kaneh-bosm | 3 |
| Atonement | 4 |
| Felt | 6 |
| Perennial lily | 8 |
| Aloe | 10 |
| Path | 11 |
| Eyes | 12 |
| Free | 14 |
| Search | 16 |
| War | 17 |
| Just Ice | 18 |
| Reveal | 20 |
| Dimensions | 21 |
| Break | 22 |
| Heights | 23 |
| Lay | 24 |
| Lost | 25 |
| Manipulate | 26 |

| | |
|---|---:|
| Forget you | 27 |
| Truth | 28 |
| Deception | 29 |
| Distance | 31 |
| Religion of love | 33 |
| Life | 34 |
| Ambivalence | 36 |
| Let us | 39 |
| My Dearest Dear | 40 |
| My habitation | 41 |
| Has someone ever made you cry? | 42 |
| Breathe | 44 |
| End of time | 45 |
| Vision | 46 |
| What's love? | 47 |
| Taste | 49 |
| Lonely candle | 51 |
| Bitter-sweet | 52 |
| Death | 53 |
| My Atonement | 54 |
| Help | 56 |
| Unfair judgement | 57 |
| Our love is fertile | 58 |
| Homeless | 59 |
| Chambre des chasse | 60 |
| Tackled | 61 |
| Today | 62 |
| Scared | 64 |

| | |
|---|---|
| Perfection | 65 |
| Decrypted End | 67 |
| Fee | 69 |
| Demon's glory | 71 |
| Sweet | 72 |
| **Truth** | 73 |
| Recipes | 74 |
| Peace | 75 |
| Gifted curse | 76 |
| Smile | 78 |
| Poison from hunger | 80 |
| Testament | 82 |
| Sentenced | 85 |
| Amen | 86 |
| Terror | 88 |
| About Author | 91 |

# Alpha bet

*Appreciation for meeting the perfect moment*

*Bee that savors the sweet, one favors the most*

*Contemplations of the first-time I called*

*Desires to let free, discipline sets an inextricable stall*

*Enchanted by kinetic emotions*

*Feng shui gives the upper hand, seeking no more from the deck*

*Guardian of a prized treasure*

*Harnessing the moment of truth*

*Inside every contemplation an inviolable spirit stands*

*Justifying thoughts within thoughts*

*Kaleidoscope of happiness*

*Lamenting on getting more*

*Narcissistic behavior in overdrive*

*Obligated to the win or lose, anecdote*

*Passionate inquisitions plagued by insecurities*

*Quenched by lust*

*Resistance to conform*

*Strategist to extricate temptation*

*Turning the cards, to set the pace*

*Understanding my thoughts and action*

*Victory within the journey*

*Winning the queen's heart with my spade*

*Xenolithic love, unorthodox therapy*

*Yearning for more, tokens of effort leaves one*

*Zoning by the moments to be all in*

# Kaneh-bosm

*Sacred yet hated*

*Truth manipulated to hide you from the multitude*

*Aromatic peace. the only altitude*

*Framed by many but never seen in the picture*

*Painting an image portraying you as being so bitter*

*The euphoria of knowledge, the roots of wisdom*

*The key hidden within exodus*

*Clef de voûte of the truth*

*See the oracular third eye they tried to blind*

*Foundation of all, let one see within the inner tent*

*Imprisoned for possessing the freedom to life*

*Covenant of civilization*

*I am*

*Hidden by many to gain wealth*

*The cure for all*

# Atonement

*I atone on behalf of my gender*

*Sorry for the tears and sleepless nights*

*Hours of not caring or treating you right*

*I failed, I faded I dimmed your light*


*I atone on behalf of my race*

*Stumbling on hurdles, the pain in freedom songs*

*We ran and fought for way too long*

*Forgive me for the past hate and tribulations, I humbly share the wrong*


*I atone on behalf of humanity*

*Where the selfless charm of vanity favors*

*I abused and ignored the laws of nature*

*I killed, I murdered I hated on the land's failure*


*Sorry for the many excuses*

*I'm sorry for being just man*

# Felt

*Sunny lands filled with smile and joy*

*There came the thunder raining spoils*

*It's just a game, it's just a toy*

*Through the dim one secretly toils*

*The midst of darkness erupting coy*


*Eyes thereof wonder, lusting desires steals one's skin*

*towards the weak insecurity ponders fear*

*Robbing of innocence, the temptations of sin*

*Emotions seeming less, to whom do they care?*

*A gamble of loyalty to which desires win*


*Rich as argile molded to play*

*Hysteria ambushes and rapes the lustful mind*

*thoughts dim the lights of happiness' stay*

*perspective of trust scars and leaves one blind*

*history masked by the hands of clay*


*tricyclic pedaling anhedonia, a day of blurry vision*

*trusted hands molds neuroticism as just*

*deceived by thunder, a playful mission*

*the times thereof deduction is a plus*

*multiplying hate an equal division*

# Perennial lily

*A mother's touch, a mother's care*

*Take my hands; let me wipe your tears*

*I see your pain, the wounds of a thousand spears*

*Disappointed in the perennial lily that thrived in flames*

*Blossoming in seasons of the droughty rains*


*The life of the many rays*

*Giving hope and vision in so many ways*

*Planting sweat on days of raining tears*

*The crest placed within one's chest*

*The queen that made the most from the less*


*The lily that turned tears into rain, to thrive in flames*

*I cry to your perfection giving thanks you're the best*

*Your courage and honor, one must invest*

*Planting sweat, the days of raining tears*

*Overcoming all odds, neutralizing fears*

*Blossoming in flames of pain*

# Aloe

*Bitter but so good*

*Ignorance embraced, a tree of no wood*

*The truth within faith*

*Ignored and abandoned for the acquired taste*

*Aloe is the love I give*

*Bitter but so good*

*Lighting fires without wood*

*Purging the mind spirit and soul*

*Accepting the roots of dirt over gold*

*Bitter but no good*

*Charmed by sweets, decayed and rot*

*Illuminating world, a tree of no roots seeks a spot*

*A tree of no wood I rather be*

*Igniting fires on the ever-cold sea*

*Bitter but so good*

# Path

*Failure after failure*

*Suicidal thoughts lingering, walls to sanity stumbling*

*cessation is my test*

*Success has me puffing sess*

*The smile of worth is slowly fading*

*Is this my gift? I'm only asking*

*Medication for meditation rooted me up*

*The eye within, freer are us*

*Mental slavery the blur that's killing us bad*

*The king of deception, the ingenious plan*

*Let one be free, as genuine dies young*

*Plants of upliftment hidden from the sun*

*Lies become factual, the truth being lies*

*Chains reflecting sugar cane and cotton, unforgettable times*

*Napoleon shot the face but couldn't kill the race*

*Life runs on one track, we all running the same race*

# Eyes

*Million eyes opened in darkness*

*One eye opened in the moment of light*

*Silver and gold shekels walk in elegance on the dreary waters at night*

*Silver streaks jog slowly in the midst*

*Kissing the whispers embracing the golden lips*


*Picturesque, beauty like beta lacerta*

*Spirits, beauty and souls on a merger*

*Plush giants that bless the eyes*

*Beauty within the midst that flies*

*Silver and gold shekels walk in elegance on the dreary waters at night*


*Aura intermediately justified*

*The beauty when you open your eyes*

# Free

*When is one truly free?*

*Never forget the roots of your tree*

*Shackles on our mind and spirits*

*Where do we find our civics?*


*A prison within a prison*

*Nature tells, but when will we listen?*

*Minds blurred by the scope of no hope*

*The view of a colourless kaleidoscope*


*1843!!*

*Now we poison the roots of what was to be a blossoming tree*

*Believing others yet not believing in thy self*

*Rich but have no wealth*

*When is one truly free?*


*When one takes out his eyes and sees with his heart*

*Knowing his eyes only sees just farce*

*The fire that freezes knowledge*

*The past the future, shot by whips*

*When will your heart see?*

*when will you be free*

# Search

*Trapped within one's face*

*Demons of the air the eyes can taste*

*Lost within a mask*

*Incarcerated freedom, leaves the mind to ask*

*Fiery waters that flows through clouds of terror*

*endowed to the mirrors of error*

*Transmigration within the anti-clock*

*A door within a lock*

*A start that has no beginning, has no stop*

*The sin of the righteous*

*Peace within the unjust*

*Fiery waters that flows through clouds of terror*

*endowed to the mirrors of error*

# War

Lights of war

The shooting of constant bullets

The day when friendship turns to hate

Times when I question our fate

This is the day when there's no anancies

The day when we are troubled by the wounds of the mouth

Dignity on a low and violence decides to shout

Without any doubt

We are the compass that defines north and south

The light of our war

## Just Ice

Why cry for justice? When justice is on trial

Sentenced for life for blatant lies

On Trial for rampantly judging one's skin

Murder me! for its now a curse to have my gift

Imprisoned freedom lies in evidence

Should Justice be where we seek residence?

Peace now the polluted air, masters filter slavery

Tattoos, lyrics our everyday physics being cast away


no origin for killing the trees before it blossoms the fruit

but we remain strong as our roots

heart stabbed by the killer of art

beheaded, shot, burnt, murdered by law

justice, just ice; a cold-hearted murderer of the right

slaughtering you, killing me, beheading us

Always being unjust

For your ways will make one sin


Mark us kings still, Dreams of the insomniac

The ice that freezes knowledge

Freedom with shackles and fences

# Reveal

*Your heart is wearing a mask*

*Let me see your elegance, let not this be a farce*

*Why be afraid, to show who you truly are?*

*Beneath there's make-up, that hides who you are*

*There's braveness hiding with courage*

*A satellite that's afraid to feed the world with it's ever known coverage*

*Reveal your constant beauty*

*Rest assure, as the sea swallows the sun slowly*

*My love will smash that mask*

*Letting your light glow*

*True beauty and elegance, now being your only task*

*Make-up will decay but you will forever last*

# Dimensions

*When I die, I will search all of eternity just for you*

*One shouldn't be scared because my heart and soul awaits for you*

*Let me be reincarnated by your enchanting love*

*Let the love that I've died for give me life*

*Make not the hands of time be retroverted*

*But indeed, let my future heart enter yours*

*Ever yet contradicting the meaning of hate*

*Hating your smile because it sends me in the midst of time*

*When I die, our love will grow to secluded dimensions*

*Our thoughts bringing forth synchronized intentions*

*let me be reincarnated by your enchanting love*

# Break

*We are the sand that makes the glass*

*Now we ask time, will our love ever last?*

*So fragile I wonder if we'll break*

*Like the time for lunch for you I ache*


*The hour glass I beg to be spared*

*Limitation of time is what I have always feared*

*Sometimes I wish to smash my past*

*Living in a world that is made of glass*


*Everything seems so hard but breaks so easily*

*As lightening comes, we bond to be stronger at our weakest state*

*A time for eternal awakening*

*We are the sand that makes the glass*

*The future fate of the past*

# Heights

*My words lost of wind because they don't blow your mind*

*Defying nature for falling in spring*

*Leaves that cuddle and kiss with the endless wind*

*The trees whistle while the birds sing*


*I lust at your blessing knowing I have sinned*

*The sky jealous of the level of our love*

*The renaissance of my heart, has made me hungry for love. Eating the wind*

*Mountains jealous of the peak of our love*


*Legacy bricks the dynasty from blood*

*Reaching for the heights of love*

# Lay

*My lady lay with me I plea*

*Your smile is the sun that wakes with me*

*From the womb to the tomb you're in love with thee*

*Needing to spend time you are my only currency*


*You and me making us the hypothesis of a relationship*

*Never needing to dock we always set sail*

*Algebraic expressions "u", "n", "i" makes every algorithm great*

*We are the key signatures to the rhythm of love*


*The emotions that emote the greatest feel*

*"Uni" meaning we are one*

*From the womb to the tomb you're in love with thee*

*The love that brings melody*


*My lady lay with me*

# Lost

*Light of darkness is where I seek refuge*

*Enlightened by the black lights thou is enthused*

*The moment where rage and hate conquers*

*All lights out, darkness rules the dominion*

*Trees wither and souls gone*

*Eaten by man's hunger for power and fame*

*The tears of mankind that cries no shame*

*Love hiding in the gutters because of the raining pain*

*Lies, deceit and hate is our now love*

*There is a darker light within waiting to be revealed*

*Let that light shine beyond these walls*

*Enlightened by the black lights thou is enthused*

*Darkness the light, the man of sight*

# Manipulate

*You love the darkness within me*

*Wanting me to be the old man I see*

*Scared but safe, scared of the demons I attain*

*Hating it, loving the sensation it brings*

*I'm your heaven and hell, Psychedelic thoughts, Utopian laws*

*Safe within my arms*

*Pain of pleasure, the pleasure of loving pain*

*Desires of fantasies one now paints*

*Hating love, loving hate*

*Doctor of pain, a rust of the most glorious gates*

*Joy and happiness, sweet memoirs*

*Councilor, a friend, me amor*

# Forget you

*I wish to have amnesia, to forget the times we had*

*This is the beauty*

*The cliché of being sad*

*We are the sea without flora, the seas without sand*

*Only memories and dreams as to where we stand*


*It's been years I haven't seen you while awake*

*Blind me from within*

*No more dreams, no great lakes*

*Disable my senses to forget your taste*

*No beginning forfeiting the race*


*I wish to have amnesia, to forget the times we had*

*Purge by the ugly truth*

*I wish to forget the sad*

*Sentimental days, when we had our plan*

*The earth has quaked, shivering our land*

# Truth

*If I was any much younger I would say*

*Roses are red, violets are blue*

*Our love is unstoppable because it is true*

*Now am old enough to say*

*Your love is my light, you are my breath, my optimistic sight*

*Now am bold enough to know*

*No matter what I say I can't express how much I truly adore you*

*As silly as it may sound, my emotions for you can't be told*

*To tell you how I feel only God he knows*

*To tell the true story of love it's us he chose*

*With humble elegance you are my distinctive rose*

# Deception

*In the lots of darkness, you have slowly gone*

*Destroying and Smashing, every light is now extinct, forever gone*

*Who are you?*

*A person I know not no more*

*Blocking out every light, a door without a key-hole*

*Not a sneak peep nothing to grasp, nothing to hold*

*Façade is at its best*

*Deception to the inner true self*

*Who am I?*

*A person I know not no more*

*A sea without sand, a sea without any shore*

*Wanting to know have I strayed?*

*Have I strayed into the lions' den?*

*Show me light, give me me, my true and unquestionable self*

# Distance

*We are like the stars and the moon*

*No matter how far we place ourselves there's still a connection.*

*But as Shakespeare says "the true course of love never did run smooth"*

*I open my eyes and realize you're my heart's only soothe*

*As fate predicts friends we are, friends we shall be.*

*I contemplate on my infinite love that could blossom into a prolific tree*


*Trapped within my heart waiting to be cared for waiting to be freed*

*A strong a woman, a future mom that's intelligent and bold*

*You're a priceless possession, my future goal*

*Here is our story, the true meaning of the depths of love that has never yet been told*

*Not afraid yet fearful to love*

*Your desirable charm makes the heart lust*


*Forces me to love you endlessly from flesh continuing at ash and dust*

*Jealous are they that seek us to make a fuss*

*Very strong are we that fell very weakly in love*

*Feeling free like a newly flying dove.*

# Religion of love

*Eternal love is what I preach*

*Learning to be a true lover to the world I teach*

*Love is my life, love is my religion*

*A true missionary of your sanctifying heart, hoping never to once depart*

*Speaking the words of truth, you my root, the beat of soothe*

*An Angelic-being who is captured in the depths of my heart*

*The ambassador of the religion of love is who I am*

*Learning more about love is my aspiring plan*

*Eternal love is what I preach*

*I give you my heart for taking, can you reach?*

*Be my gospel my testament to life*

*Ignore the congregation of lies*

*Pure as the holy water one testifies*

*The truth in all your why's*

# Life

*We are more than love, we are life*

*We are biochemicals fused to give what's called love*

*The heart, the breath, the moments of life we symbolize*

*Others follow to thee they idolize*


*Like electricity and bulb, we give sight*

*Infinite love being our eternal light*

*Constantly reciprocating love at its best*

*We give our hearts till the day we lay to rest*


*We are love and so much more*

*Giving life to love while we love our lives*

*Within darkness we made light*

*For you and our love I'll always fight*


*Take my eyes, the sacrifice of love*

*The strength within our weakness makes the foundation*

*Blinded by beauty the eyes that sees no temptation*

*We are more than love, we are life*

## Ambivalence

*Hating love because it hates me*

*Condemning life because it condemns me*

*Erasing u from us because you erased me*

*I die to live while I live to die*

*Should I tell the truth? Should I lie?*

*Should I laugh? Should I cry?*


*Knowing the game doesn't change it's only the players*

*Wondering when to love, when to play?*

*Will this night bring a brighter day?*

*Questions I know not an answer to*

*Paranoid by the meaning of love*

*Hating your presence, loving your company*

*Moments wishing you'd come for me*


*Here patiently waiting for an answer*

*Just take my breath away, be my cancer*

*I love…*

*I don't believe in love*

*Drugs the replacement for sentimental hugs*

*Holy water consuming my lungs and blood*

*Beyond the call, duty perks homicide's aid*

*the dirt consumed where reality fades*

# Why???

*Living in a world of only questions, I contemplate why?*

*Why so many innocent people have to die?*

*Why hunger and starvation is our daily cry?*

*Why do we always judge and never yet self-examine our harrowing lives?*

*Is the world ignoring to answer us?*

*These are few questions needed to be acknowledged*

*Without questions where is truth? Enlighten my knowledge*

*Without answers aren't we married to a world of savage?*

*Contemplate!*

*Help me ask why?*

*Why the seven deadly sins talk to us?*

*Why happiness cries and a smile dies?*

*What would the world be without a lie?*

*They always say curiosity kills the cat*

*Is napoleon great because he shot the black?*

*Why do we have to attack the race because the race attacked?*

*Why is it a crime to be just black*

# Let us

*Let us be a choir*

*Let us raise the pitch a little higher*

*Make us in being a storm*

*Let us create devastation by doing no harm*

*Let us create a topping with our past being the crust*

*We should be metal, which creates no reason to rust*

*Give a million meanings of love and they all come back to us*

*Let our hearts be jointly endeavored in lust*

*Unbreakable we are that's a plus*

*Let us be the tree of life*

*Skip all the talks because they all symbolize the infallible and imperfect us*

## My Dearest Dear

*Mesmerizing eyes a thoughtful cheer*

*Your heated smile my heart wishes to wear*

*The unending meaning of humble elegance*

*Makes one going crazy be of inevitable relevance*

*The masterpiece of masterpieces I must confess*

*Molding and carving the man I am*

*Creating my days, months and years*

*Disappointing you causing countless tears*

*I will make you proud one day I say*

*To be a better man scars my knee, the way I pray*

*The love of my life*

*My alpha, my dearest dear*

# My habitation

*My haven, my home*

*My heavenly dome*

*Me in your heart as a crystal, your foundation stone*

*I live to cherish my kingdom*


*I stand to watch me the king of my palace*

*Me to you like Christians to their chalice*

*Conquering your heart by failing numerous conquests*

*My queen, my honor*

*My heart salutes yours*


*From now till the end loving you is all I intend*

*Domiciled in your heart*

*A queen so smart*

*A native within the eyes, a refuge when the sky cries, intense beauty*

*A haven for when the heart dies, the place of no lies*

*My haven, my home*

## Has someone ever made you cry?

*Has someone ever made you cry?*

*Something so special has slowly died*

*Two picnic years, 739 nights*

*something of great altitude has lost its magnificent heights*

*All seems like not the best*

*Winning the war losing the test*

*Always competing even when there's no contest*

*Fights on fights, care fatigued and left me alone*

*Heated days on the raining battlefield*

*Losing hope because faith can't cope*

*Me winning sadness and eternal pain*

*Heart cries with blooded eyes*

*Now its sadness turned into joy*

*Waters that stitch the broken*

*Regards of death as a token*

*The sensation of tomorrow you have pain*

*Has someone ever made your sky rain?*

# Breathe

*You gave me the breath, when I couldn't breathe*

*Gave me hope when I couldn't cope*

*Visioning rainbows when there's a terrible storm*

*me climbing this unending slope*


*Once I see your smile there's hope of a better day*

*A day when we will be together till eternity I say*

*Time stops as I breathe once more*

*As the feeling of true love enters my core*

*Undeniably what I feel is pure*

*The truth of joy we can endure*


*Your carbon my oxygen*

*Reciprocation of exchange till the end*

*I breathe your breath once more*

# End of time

*Stabbing me violently, breaking my wings*

*Slowly every light starts to dim*

*How will I ever learn to fly?*

*A question I ask of you, the one*

*I stop the clock to reach the end of time*

*No more soul music I've kill every chime*

*What's the reason to live if I cannot fly?*

*A gruesome murderer who left me to die*

*No tears as I wish not to cry*

*My wings flatter and I stumble as I wish to fly*

*I smash the hourglass to meet the end of time*

*How will I ever fly and live so free?*

*I wish to fly*

*Fly to meet the ends of time*

# Vision

*If my heart could see then love wouldn't be blind*

*If you were my brain then you would know why, then you wouldn't mind*

*If my eyes could talk then I could describe how beautiful you are*

*Minds lapping their hands making love to the twinkling star*


*Let me see within and read your mindless thoughts*

*What if I tell the lies of truth?*

*Harness my feet and mute my mouth*

*Let my eyes walk and talk, my mind touching your geographical spots north and south*


*Let me be your window, the place you seek peace, your tranquil view*

*Whisper in my heart and say I love you*

*Kiss my eyes with your senseless beauty*

## What's love?

*Love, just a four-lettered word many use in vain*

*But my pores embedded by that thread, I feel happiness, I feel pain*

*Electricity like muddy waters flowing through my veins*

*your charm enthused by magnifying beauty, slowly driving me insane*

*Do you believe in love?*

*The act of a dove's feather being corvus*

*The greatest feeling of feelings coming from within*

*What else could love be?*

*The deepest contemplation, you sharing my lung*

*The Shui to my Feng*

*An illusion of the heart to sing a song we never yet sung*

*Kindred spirits dancing in the garment of the young*

*I do love, I feel happiness, I feel pain*

*I feel the sunshine within the rain*

*The demons within an angel walks among*

*The heaven within hell that lusts not of righteousness*

*do you believe in love?*

*Do you believe in me?*

# Taste

*Lips soft and cushioned with love, a taste of peace, birds flying above*

*Trees shiver, the mild wet dew, branches fondle the climaxed air*

*Butterflies wild in delight to the clouds they climb*

*Savagely devouring peace, stroking delight*

*Mountains moved, electricity ignite*

*Angelic tunes in sync to the room of light*

*Fire beetles sets the day in night*

*Sensational bliss souls so perfect connect and kiss like north and south*

*River banks flood whilst volcanoes erupt*

*Tranquille feel of feathers induced by the feeling of heaven's gate opening*

*Pleasure exceeding the limits*

*Journey on to the stream of fun*

*The missionary in perspective, a voyage on the rough seas*

*Humidity of the clouds kisses with chills*

*Embracing the bad, setting free the beast*

*A taste of nature's pudding*

# Lonely candle

*Taken away in the midst of joy and friendship*

*A lonely candle in the wind blown out way too soon*

*Your light gone but your true essence never left the atmosphere*

*For a true and loving friend I honestly care*


*My heart has been torn apart with anguish, loneliness and fear*

*Where will I ever find someone like you?*

*Take me with you, put me to endless sleep with a poisoned spear*

*Please I ask save me the tear*


*Your joyful peace I will willing share*

*Utopia for me to see you again is nearing soon*

*As destined to die is no longer my fear.*

# Bitter-sweet

*Bitter-sweet it is losing you my love*

*You've found happiness and new love*

*But my endless tears and pain won't do much good*

*As the flames of my heart are thirsty for wood*

*I need you more than ever*

*I cry through the storm in the sunny weather*

*Happy am I to see you smile by charms*

*Gone away never to return in my hospitable arms*

*I awake as your heart alarms signifying my heart is no longer in yours*

*Melting my epidermis and crushing my core*

*Telling me you love me no more*

*You've found happiness and new love*

*Bitter-sweet it is losing you my love*

# Death

*I have died once before and I feel my end is nearing once more*

*So cold my lungs breathe a sigh of goodbye*

*Suddenly decapitated left to see not the narrowing light*

*Not without a chance to know two wrongs don't make a right*

*My eyes close as the sun sets losing a non negotiable fight*

*Hands and legs slashed apart left me an amputee*

*Crying for forgiveness as you ignore my thought provoking plea*

*It's too late now I have figured its omega as I lie*

*Ribs torn apart as life sails away*

*Away to a far away land where love has forbidden I*

*Archaic heart so cold heats the dark*

*my heavens pack it's bags*

*As I watch true love die with me*

## My Atonement

*This is my atonement to you*

*My heart aches so I know it's overdue*

*It's a lie what they all say*

*I feel permanent pain and temporary joy*

*Am sorry for lowering you into a painful decoy*


*Please forgive me for causing so much terror*

*Save your tears I will make no more error*

*You deserve the best of me*

*One like you shouldn't have fallen*

*Causing you pain was the only joy I could see*


*Now I see I am always wrong*

*I wish for change*

*To tuck you in at nights and sing you a lullaby song*

*Got you under hypnosis is no longer my range*


*I treasure your heart more than ever*

*Forgive me please because I knew not my error*

# Help

*I only have 'my' because I've lost the self that was once within*

*Help me to find that self, help me to be myself once more*

*A man without blood, a man without veins*

*Locked away, buried alive, plastered with locks and cherished with chains*

*Fearing the light because of living in the dark*

*When will I ever learn to love an iridescent spark?*

*Strong as a hart yet my heart is weak*

*Redemption once a foe but it's you I seek*

*To walk in the park and find myself is all I need*

*For as to cut me there's no blood I need myself to bleed*

*Help me to find that self, help me to find me*

## Unfair judgement

*Judge me not because of my past*

*Practice it was to perfect my task*

*For I tell you you're my contemplation, my heart*

*Brighter than the sun, my deepest warmth*

*Such a beauty doing your duty, creating unjustifiable haunt*

*Asking for one's love but no you can't*

*My practice has left me a failure*

*A cloth thrown away from it's tailor for its contemplative perfection*

*Painting a picture of promiscuity wasn't my intention*

*Doing greatness only leaves one in detention*

*What should be my conception?*

*Judge me not because of my past*

*Practice it was to perfect my task*

## Our love is fertile

*Dirt and time, fertile and worthwhile*

*Beauty and elegance, vision and humbled*

*Troubled with the curse of being a captivating subjugator*

*Giving life to every breadth*

*We breathe your air, we breathe your breath*


*A lover, a mom, a friend*

*Immortality and longevity is your name*

*Cliché it is to say I love you and call your name*

*Your heart is in mine without doubt not in vein*


*Our love is fertile*

*Needing to spend time is my currency*

*Giving life to every breadth*

*We breathe your air, we breathe your breath*

Homeless

*Hate seeks refuge in mortality*

*You are my love, my immortality*

*A homeless heart veined with pain*

*The source of life within death*

*Desires to conjugate pain with pain*

*Smile that rises in the east and sets at west*

*Embracing Death within death*

*Loving the wrongs within the right*

*Seeing love for being blind*

*Searching knowing there's nothing to find*

*Thoughts concluded only in the mind*

## Chambre des chasse

*love has left me a homeless heart*

*memories ending without a start*

*infatuation creating chambre des chasse*

*weighing heavily yet no mass*

*the courage to be discouraged by façade*

*darkness the means of illumination*

*cloned by degradation, the air of sensational suffocation*

*gravity of love defied, truth being lied*

*inevitability being subliminal impossibility*

*infatuation creating chambre de chasse*

*weighing heavily yet no mass*

*indentation on a wall of no walls*

*Love has left me a homeless heart*

# Tackled

*Words of silence, motionless actions*

*Transparency turning opaque*

*Given without a take*

*An ocean in just a bottle*

*Formidable whispers caused by endless tears*

*Approaching the monster giving me fears*

*Tackled by bravery deducing, ending mental slavery*

*Once trapped by charm*

*Extricated from harm*

*Once a prisoner of freedom*

*Formidable whispers caused by endless tears*

*Seeing beneath the mask one wears*

Today

*Apate justified in being eros*

*The glittery roads abused by emptiness we encompass*

*Doves enthused by friendly scarecrows*

*The Mirage of an aeon kindred spirit has pass*

*Lost within souls a smile further than atlas' celestial vows*

*The unwanted colours dance on a prestigious canvas as to where they fade*

*Charmed by the head of Echidna, whilst typhon ignites life brighter than the stars, yet erebus fearful of my shade*

*The underworld is Utopia garnished with strife*

*Kissed by Athena, tricked by Apate as deception is made*

*Mirage of an aeon kindred spirit*

*Light compromised by the eyes of darkness*

*Hate cultivated by love and harvested in death*

*Cronus losing watch as the flock craves to be enslaved*

*What is forever?*

*What is time today?*

# Scared

*How many times can a heart heal?*

*Anhedonia restricting the lands of the sky*

*A human septum embracive of corroding connections*

*Deception kissing affections like the sun caressing the waters*

*Distance the closest neighbor of fear one resides*

*spirituality coinciding with condemnation*

*Tears of the heart contradicting the diction of peace*

*Era of most being just a pebble in the oceans*

*Heart cries while eyes bleed, the worst is now a deed*

*Glass so fragile breaking what's concrete*

*Faith decapitated, no chance of a leap*

*How many times can a heart heal?*

*Until its dead then only can it feel*

*Kinetic focused in potential, rendered not to be*

Perfection

*Thou needeth a girl that speaketh the tongue of those who seek the wildest adventures on the rough, most humored seas*

*Wherefore not from the hands of this era, thus thou lay their feet in the silvery waters reading pages of art*

*Daisies and lilies the smell of leaves on those weary days*

*Aura of chirps, wet grass a smile through the window pane*

*Fighting for love but is love for fighting?*

*Muffins and bread, fresh fruits from the hands of thy partner*

*A domicile, creating thus bond with nature as our home*

*Tender pecks on the forehead justifying thy love, the care not many of thee will harvest*

*The sombre tone of silence resonating in the sad minds*

*Picnics, dinners and lunch, A stringent path they say to divulge our love*

*Parties and lingering, I'd rather symphonies*

*Sands become one's feet, I hold thou's hand in sync to the waves lustfully riding the beach*

*I needeth a girl to see my soul within the windows that carved my pane*

*Aroma of herbs kissing my senses, as the world makes love to every ingredient*

*Sensational feel of one's soft, mesmerizing touch*

*Placing rum in the wild pines to chill whilst intaking the aura of the sun roasting grass*

*Infallible phi like a gaggle lopes in fury to engulf the fields*

*The sense of comfort through volcanic tears*

*Calibrating to compromise with sensational love only to justify*

*Thou needeth a girl that speaketh that tongue*

Decrypted End

*Truth hidden to favor love*

*Lies escape from sadness*

*Moments obliterated by the need to pretend there's peace above*

*Time the master that builds and burn the stairs of hope's madness*


*Kindred heart awakes evil like a fearful dove*


*Wandering into one's own thought*

*Cipher of Caesar, colours that make a colourless kaleidoscope*

*Ill from healing, urge to hurt*

*Will to harness pain and smile in deceit through burning flames*


*Letting loose, embracing you*


*Persuasion painting meaningless talks*

*Safety combatted by fear*

*Assets ignored by the sense of quid pro quo mileage*

*Past passing the present a tell*

- .- -.- . -.-. .- .-. .

*Omega 0f prospective Genesis*

Fee

*I'm a loser*

*A failure to mankind*

*Being real, in me that you can't find*

*Homo-sapiens driven by success*

*Rich but have no wealth*

*A disgrace it is to be just me*

*Lazy as can be*

*Failure meets happiness, as success fails to be happy*

*Unorthodox it is to be orthodox*

*Rare it is to think inside the box*

*Being me refusing to wear a mask*

*Moonrock deciphers humans aren't indeed real*

*Depression the world's therapeutic scene*

*Livers swim in dirty waters*

*Windows flood from the desired pain*

*Bloody waters stain the soul*

*The world with the real so cold*

*Prioritizing makes one fake*

*Masked parasites, aches to the real*

*I love you, the words I hate*

*Toxic it is to be just you*

*If only you were me, what would you do?*

*Isolated in seclusion, living in a world of just illusions*

*Confusion within constitutions*

*The age of promiscuous virgins, retribution a procurement*

*Trapped within my doorsteps*

*A loser am I, just living to die*

*Trying not to try*

*Losing to win*

# Demon's glory

*Touching the skins of the senseless, slithery most weary hands*

*Works of candles, a ghost of evil plans*

*Divulging innocent, one's dream as large as zaara sands*

*Lips that adulterate takes peace*


*Darkness is my solis*

*Winter is one's summery heart*

*Regaining the treasure one thought was obliterated*

*Deadly yet humble the face thou wear*

*Sinners at peace, the righteous in fear*

*Violence is my care*


*Heat of ice the sensation you bring*

*Merely thankful that I have sinned*

*Gospel of the darkness thou lips sing*

*Revelations of the demons I want to kill*

# Sweet

*Generation focused on fame, more so than staying sane*

*Morals for the clout, degradation of hope*

*Enthused by greed, a mask of a million tears*

*The face within a tear*


*Paper evolves to love, love maneuvered by paper*

*Sinners are saviours, embraced and loved*

*Poverty becomes a bank for the rich*

*A world crying from wounds and scars*


*who am I to judge? A sinner am I*

*Darkness the definition of light*

*Morals devalued, the standards of great heights*

*An ant on a kite enjoying the flights*

*The killer of dreams awakes at night.*

# Truth

*When will we realize, beauty isn't physical*
*Not subjected to cotton or oil*
*Destined we all are to till the soil*
*A pulchritude within the mind and spirit*
*Pure within the skin that ages the wine*

*The atomic particles of the taste of time*
*Obsession of energy than that of skin*
*The unwanted fruit ignored on the limb*
*Eyes determine perfection and imperfections thereof*
*Price of beauty is at a lost*

*Fake smiles while the soul cries*
*Where in one's soul does beauty lie?*
*Pulchritudinous by garments beneath the skin*
*Ugly it is to have beauty within*
*Cursed now bless like a miracle*
*The fake love that drinks with success.*

Recipes

*A slice of pain and the need for comfort, I saw and took a bite*

*Sweet honey and milk savored in richness*

*The sense to be alone with the shadows as witness*

*Wild and free never to be imprisoned by light*

*Endless talks as the pillow hears the snore*

*Hours being ours one testifies as core*

*Darkness, intense pain an iced look, the eyes looked*

*What do lies do when one is sore?*

*Reproduction breeds endless thoughts*

*Visions of where life would be*

*Happiness within arguments exceeds all doubts*

*Isolated but seen, bonded but free*

*A taste of the twelve slices of love*

# Peace

*Meet miss world*

*Looking through the scope to see the ticket away*

*A beauty it is to be dressed in gold*

*Caressed by the strong black, your only hold*

*The whisperer of dreams untold*


*True self gets pulled to reality by gravity's lust*

*Embraced and loved as she glides off the run way*

*Clap as she makes her way off*

*Hands relaxed, fingers stay calm*


*Kiss on the forehead, the true signification of love*

*Eyes closed as gold touches flesh*

*Miss world has me missing the world*

*Red carpet as she departs*

*Shìjiào says the whispers as they disseminate*

Gifted curse

*Real never attained the gift to be in flesh for too long*

*Harmonized in the melodic symphony of nature's song*

*Presence of purity infiltrates the air*

*Smile that turns memories into tears*

*Soul of the utmost tier ignored by fame*

*Rights being wrong, shortcuts- the means traveling of long*

*Heavier than the cross, the sins to carry on*

*Spiritually free, physically imprisoned*

*Whispers that cries truth one silently listens*

*Disrelish in flesh a message of hope*

*Cancer embracive of the need to cope*

*Unending contemplation of the blessed sin*

*Domiciled in revelations the mind's eye rest*

*Shackles on lucidity, freedom on the neck*

*The price for thirty sheckles*

*Truth within the weight of wait*

*Have we paid the price?*

*A curse amid the gifted, the tree that blossoms virus*

Smile

*I often wonder what the world would be without me*

*Would it place endless smiles on everyone's faces knowing am of no existence?*

*The reflection within the cat's eye*

*The truth outside the mirror*

*Am I the meaning of persistent sadness?*

*Am I living right? or am I just in a mirage?*

*The stranger within the mirror, how much do I differ?*

*holding on to a branch of just waters*

*Eternal sadness glorifies elation*

*Masked in happiness, infallible pain climaxes droughty tears*

*Knowing the lion within me died like a dehydrated plant*

*Asking the stranger, am I living right?*

*Happy will I be to grant that wish*

*Smiles on faces, here's to no pain*

*Murdering suicide, the real-life game*

*I often wonder what the world would be without me*

*Lost in the thought of being right*

*Contemplations of the difference between the reflection and me*

*Smile knowing I'm of no flesh*

*The mirror inside shattered to sand illuminating reflection of no more lies*

*Clocks blinded by nature to know I'm gone*

*Moments of better days, rejoice when my lights dim to a fall*

*For the stranger I owe, smile when I'm gone*

*I wonder if you think of me*

Poison from hunger

*Nouvelle cuisine polishes one lips*

*Wine of white, sensational bliss*

*Ghrelin and leptin the wars of fight*

*Sauté, gourmet, fueled by appetence of hunger*

*Diamond punch, aura for munches*

*Chymified by many, the horrifying crime*

*Hunger painted in sfumato, the truth within Lisa's eyes*

*Illusion of wealth. where the legion hides*

*Battle for survival, hunters of talent, Eagle's eye*

*Scavenger of deception*

*Hunger being the last supper*

*Poisoned from hunger, plethora feasts on greed*

*Heights of great men, the wisdom to lead*

*Poison sautéd in the richness of hunger*

*The key that restricts but never open*

*The mind that opens but never restrict*

*The man feasting on poverty*

Testament

*Depression the genesis of me starting to lie*

*Never dare to ignite the lamps, the truth of my exodus*

*Isolation my Leviticus, the succession am I to whom judges*

*The numbers I reminisce there on, the days I am antisocial*

*Second eye opened, it's new to thee, living everyday my Deuteronomy*

*Prosperous like Canaan, many, Joshua tells*

*Slew with Ruth anchor the arteries of my root*

*Dear o' Samuel, the generation that disregards pulp fiction*

*fighting a battle of the dome, Mozart as a skill, Rehoboam as kings*

*the chronicles of pain, intoxication the Ezra of times*

*kaneh-bosm as restoration to life like Nehemiah's leadership*

*An Esther one fails to find in a world of moral decay,*

*Love the psalm one sings to mark extrication from imprisonment*

*Job one seeks but tell recurring proverbs*

*The kohelet to life, die to live, Ecclesiastes tells*

*Breathing the songs of Solomon till I die*

*Isiah's eyes, imminent peace, spiritual sights*

*Lamentations of Jeremiah mirrors my suffering and pain*

*The ocutus of curse and blessings where amongst Ezekiel lies*

*The Daniel amid the lions*

*Lo ruhamah amongst us Hosea forsees*

*Acrididae gregariously feeding on unrighteous deeds, Joel envisions*

*Threshing transgressions Amos poetically tells*

*Deceived by the heart, setting nests amongst the stars Obadiah warns*

*Hearken like Micah envisioning a new beginning*

*A comforter like Nahum one needs in the bloody city*

*Hear me dear lord as I plea like Habakkuk*

*Consumed by the devil's water, the humble and lowly, I await Zephaniah vision*

*Kane bosm my therapeutic Haggai*

*Life injects the four horsemen within my veins, Zechariah feasts his eyes on the world's recognition*

*Unchartered roads Malachi tells me to turn back*

*Beware the ides of loyalty, Matthew tells*

*The resurrection and death Luke warms*

*Epistle to the romans as a new testament*

*Corinthians knowing not what love is*

*Sense of no matter amongst the galatians*

*Benjamin imprisoned, my art a letter to the Ephesians*

*The gifted, Peter denies*

*Revelation like Jonah's, the acts within the eye*

*Abate all lamps, slew my tears from pain*

Sentenced

*The state finds me guilty*
*Treason to the mind and soul*
*Charges of overthinking, massacre on emotions*
*The need to not be bold*
*Witnessed but not seen*

*Defendant of many personalities, having concealed no solidarity*
*Capital punishment enchants to pay a fine*
*Sentenced to chains and shackles on the mind*
*Imprisoned in amygdala, the depths of no return*
*Sadness my happiness, the table that will never turn*

*Pills and liquor subdue bailiffs detention*
*Different faces affirm, emotions unheard*
*The state finds depression guilty*
*A jump suits me best*
*Confessions to the magistrate of emotions*
*The state feeding pavulon potions*

Amen

*Eternal father, graciously I stand*

*Thankful for the breath within ever breadth I trod*

*Appreciative of the gift of living*

*A mind contemplative of the knowledge within*

*Forgive my presence, I have sinned*

*The master of feelings and thoughts, enlighten my darkness*

*Sanctify my heart*

*Purge my soul, increase your presence within me*

*A soul sold for whom to keep*

*Shed light in the vanta streets, your glory my peace*

*For the righteous has cast the first stone*

*Let your grace be the path I trod*

*Your love the genesis of my uprising and fall*

*Instill within me the discipline to love my neighbor*

*The heart and eyes to ignore the road of many*

*I thank you for the journey and lessons within each day*

*Be my guardian and that of one's I love*

*Protect the nations confused by greed*

*Heal the minds of the poor, as the story of wealth is ignored*

*Continue to bless me with love, knowledge and truth*

*Unlock the third eye to acknowledge and ignore the forbidden fruit*

*I give you thanks, in your name I pray*

*Amen.*

Terror

*Interrogation of self-murder*

*Focused on the tar, looking down at the burner*

*Voices masked, faces unheard of*

*Terror ponders in day, raindrops at night*

*Forgive my darkness for seeing the light*

*Irony of fighting for peace*

*Light of darkness in plain sight*

*Fuck the world!*

*The loyal being fake, out take becomes intake*

*Love defines hate*

*Confusion of understanding, ignorance being knowledge*

*Trust? the game never to be played*

*The cure is poison*

*Demons the stalkers of the known*

*Lost in the eyes never to be seen*

*Imprisoned by freedom, the mask of the earth*

*What is the price of worth?*

*Problem to one the solution to the next*

*Conclusion to why many lives take rest?*

*Trusting traitors tells honest lies*

*Tears tear the walls of truth*

*Extraterrestrial being humane*

*Voices masked, faces unheard of*

*Just be nice, brainwashed into servants*

*Let me die*

*I monetize thee O dearest*

*Love is within the soil thus the root of eternity's evil*

*I curse you*

*Blessings are for thou the weakest links that sayeth they are thou men*

*Real is the man that embraces his feet in the land of descended angels*

*Tranquil contemplations, isolation for the fake that seeks not to be great*

*Idolizing thou that is in debt within thou most glorious mask*

*Death ponders the glorification of prestige fame*

*Debt the gain, win to lose the era we choose to envision*

*The lamp that lights the mornings grace thou treasure*

*The greatest deception of all time?*

*Fabrication is one's spoken gospel*

*Reality painted with delusion*

About Author

*P. S. Harrison, born on July 29th 1995 in the parish of Manchester, Jamaica, always found peace by writing descriptive pieces. An alumni of deCarteret College Harrison was obsessed with writing and improving his vocabulary to reach aspiring goals as to be a prominent poet and writer overall. Challenges of being an introvert slowed the pace of progression as he thought himself to being an old soul and not as in tuned to the technologically social world. Writing and only sharing with friends and family with the continual feedback of "you are deep", He found the courage to share his first emotional master-piece, 'Poetic Plague' with hopes of the world appreciating his writing.*

Made in the USA
Middletown, DE
30 April 2024